CATHOLIC EDUCATION
IN THE LIGHT OF VATICAN II AND *LAUDATO SI'*

Dermot A. Lane is Parish Priest of Balally in Dublin 16. He is
retired President of Mater Dei Institute of Education, DCU.
He is author of *Stepping Stones to Other Religions: A Christian
Theology of Inter-Religious Dialogue* (2011) and *Religion and
Education: Reimagining the Relationship* (2013) and editor of
Vatican II in Ireland, Fifty Years on (2015).

CATHOLIC EDUCATION

IN THE LIGHT OF VATICAN II AND *LAUDATO SI'*

DERMOT A. LANE

VERITAS

Published 2015 by
Veritas Publications
7-8 Lower Abbey Street
Dublin 1, Ireland
publications@veritas.ie
www.veritas.ie

ISBN 978 1 84730 662 3

10 9 8 7 6 5 4 3 2 1

A catalogue record for this book is available from the British Library.

Designed by Heather Costello, Veritas Publications
Printed by eprint Ltd, Dublin

Veritas books are printed on paper made from the wood pulp of managed
forests. For every tree felled, at least one tree is planted, thereby renewing
natural resources.

CONTENTS

PART THREE
THE IMPLICATIONS OF *LAUDATO SI'* FOR EDUCATION

PART FOUR
TOWARDS A RENEWED ANTHROPOLOGY

ABBREVIATIONS, DATES AND VOTES OF COUNCIL DOCUMENTS

SC: *Sacrosanctum Concilium*, Constitution on the Sacred Liturgy, 4 December 1963: 2147 in favour, 4 against

IM: *Inter Mirifica*, Decree on the Mass Media, 4 December 1963: 1960 in favour, 164 against

LG: *Lumen Gentium*, Dogmatic Constitution on the Church, 21 November 1964: 2134 in favour, 10 against

UR: *Unitatis Redintegratio*, Decree on Ecumenism, 21 November 1964: 2137 in favour, 11 against

PC: *Perfectae Caritatis*, Decree on the Up-to-date Renewal of Religious Life, 28 October 1965: 2325 favour, 4 against

CD: *Christus Dominus*, Decree on the Pastoral Office of Bishops in the Church, 28 October 1965: 2319 in favour, 1 against

GE: *Gravissimum Educationis*, Declaration on Christian Education, 28 October 1965 : 2290 in favour, 35 against

NA: *Nostra Aetate*, Declaration on the Relation of the Church to Non-Christian Religions, 28 October 1965: 2221 in favour, 88 against

OP: *Optatam Totius*, Decree on the Training of Priests, 28 October 1965: 2318 in favour, 3 against

DV: *Dei Verbum*, Dogmatic Constitution on Divine Revelation, 18 November 1965: 2,344 in favour, 6 against

AA: *Apostolicam Actuositatem*, Decree on the Apostolate of Lay People, 18 November 1965: 2340 in favour, 2 against.

OE: *Orientalium Ecclesiarum*, Decree on Catholic Eastern Churches, 21 November 1965: 2110 in favour, 39 against

PO: *Presbyterorium Ordinis*, Decree on the Ministry and Life of Priests, 7 December 1965: 2390 in favour, 70 against

DH: *Dignitatis Humanae*, Declaration on Religious Liberty, 7 December 1965: 2,308 in favour, 4 against

AG: *Ad Gentes*, Decree on the Missionary Activity of the
        Church, 7 December 1965, 2,394 in favour, 5 against

GS: *Gaudium et Spes*, Pastoral Constitution on the Church
        in the Modern World, 7 December 1965; 2,309 in
        favour, 75 against.

INTRODUCTION

This short text sets out to mark the fiftieth anniversary of the publication of the little known *Decree on Christian Education* (1965) at the Second Vatican Council and to signal some of the educational implications of the encyclical *Laudato Si': On Care For Our Common Home* (2015).

There have been many other important developments in Catholic education in Ireland in recent times that should be noted. These include the establishment by the Irish Episcopal Conference and the Conference of Religious of Ireland of *Catholic Schools Partnership* (2010); the publication by the Irish Episcopal Conference of *Share the Good News: National Directory for Catechesis in Ireland* (2010); and the issuing by the Episcopal conference of the *Catholic Preschool and Primary Religious Education Curriculum for Ireland* (2015). Also of ongoing significance for Catholic education is the publication by John Coolahan, Caroline Hussey and Fionnuala Kilfeather of *The Forum on Patronage and Pluralism: Report of the Advisory Group* (2012) and the follow-up document from that report entitled *Progress to date and Future Directions* (2014).[1] These developments are beyond the limited scope

---

1. Both of these documents are available online at www.education.i.e.

of this particular paper; given their importance they deserve a separate treatment and that would require more than a short book.

Lying behind all of these developments is the presence of a theology of education, more often than not unspoken. Part of the purpose of this paper is to articulate the theology of education implicit in these developments by going back to the influence of Vatican II. It is hoped that this short text might shed light on the many conversations currently taking place concerning the challenges facing Catholic education in the twenty-first century.

This paper, divided into four parts, sets out to trace some of the theological shifts in Catholic Education that have taken place in the light of the Second Vatican Council (1962-1965). The first examines what developments took place at Vatican II and how these affect our understanding of Catholic education. Secondly, the paper explores a particular reading of the signs of the times offered by the Canadian philosopher Charles Taylor and how this reading throws up searching questions around anthropology. Part three considers the educational implications of *Laudato Si'*. The concluding section outlines the shape of a new anthropology in the service of Catholic education and theology.

The underlying concern of the paper is anthropology and the need for a renewed anthropology as something of singular importance to the future of Catholic education. There are of course other equally important challenges facing Catholic education. I am highlighting anthropology because I see it as a storm-centre of Catholic teaching and learning in the twenty-first century.

Anthropology is literally about the study of the human in all its complexity. Part of that complexity relates to the theological dimension of what it means to be human, which is sometimes called theological anthropology. Anthropology touches on a wide range of subjects: ecology, ethics, the meaning of marriage, the relationship between the human and the divine, original sin, gender studies, redemption, nature and grace. In a sense, anthropology, therefore, is at the centre of Catholic Education and can no longer be taken for granted. This book opens up some of the anthropological questions facing religious education and theology in the twenty-first century.

PART ONE
FRUITS OF THE SECOND VATICAN COUNCIL (1962–1965)

a. Vatican II after Fifty Years

In the light of many studies of the Council, historical and theological, it is clear that the texts of Vatican II are best interpreted in the light of the whole. By the whole, I mean in light of the conciliar process, the approved documents, and the reception of the Council. There is now broad agreement that without a grasp of the overall vision of the Council the individual documents are in danger of being inflated or manipulated for ideological ends.

There have been many different interpretations of Vatican II in the last fifty years. We do not need to repeat the history of these conflicting interpretations. Instead we have moved beyond the sterile debates of continuity versus change, via Pope Benedict's 'hermeneutic of reform', to a more integrated, holistic approach to the Council. This integrated approach suggests we should take a 'synthetic approach' to the documents,[2] while others emphasise the importance of 'a comprehensive interpretation of the Council and its documents' suggesting that the Council is more than its documents.[3] Still others suggest that the Council texts together should be seen as a new 'constitution' for the Church.[4]

Taking an aerial view of the Council allows us to discover the seminal ideas, the larger patterns, and the paradigm shifts

2. Richard Gaillardetz, 'Vatican II's Noncompetitive Theology of the Church', *Louvain Studies*, 2012: 547-569.

3. Ormond Rush, 'Towards a Comprehensive Interpretation of the Council and its documents', *Theological Studies*, 2012: 547-569.

4. Peter Hünermann, 'Der text: Werden-Gestalt-Bedeutung: Eine hermeneutische Reflexion' Herder *Theologischer Kommentar zum Zweiten Vatikanischen Konzil*, ed. P. Hünermann and B. J. Hilberath, Freiburg: Herder, 2006, V, 5-101.

that took place following the Council.[5] It is this overall vision of Vatican II that should inform our understanding of Catholic education in the twenty-first century. Up to now the approach taken was largely an analysis of individual documents without sufficient attention to the bigger picture of the Council. While a critical analysis of individual texts has its own importance, nonetheless the particularity of a document should be located within the larger context of what was happening during the conciliar period of four years. This applies especially to the *Declaration on Christian Education* which, compared to other documents, received little enough debate on the floor of the Council. Further, when that debate on education ran into controversy, it was more often agreed that the matter should be dealt with in the post-conciliar period.

b. Structural Shifts at Vatican II

What is necessary, therefore, for an informed understanding of Catholic education is a summary of some of the seminal ideas that emerged at the Council. Our summary of the significant shifts will be quite general and the selection shall be influenced by those aspects that are directly related to Catholic education. The following represents a shorthand summary of significant structural shifts:

- the adoption of a new relationship of openness by the Catholic Church towards the modern world, especially in *Gaudium et Spes.*
- a presentation of this new relationship between the Church and the modern world in terms of a call to

---

5. Giles Routier, 'Vatican II: Relevance and Future', *Theological Studies*, September 2013: 537-554 at 541.

dialogue (*GS*, 92,44) and mutuality (40-44 and 58)

- a recognition that the Church is called to a new dialogue with other Christian Churches (UR,4,9,19, 21 and 23)
- a new appreciation of the existence 'of elements of truth and grace' (AG,9) as well as the presence of 'seeds of the Word'(AG,11 and 15) in other religions(NA,2)
- a move from a propositional view of revelation to a more personal and dialogical understanding of revelation(DV, 2 and 4)
- a new appreciation of the importance of history and the emergence of a historical consciousness as a key to understanding the human (*GS*,4-5)
- a shift from a deductive, a historical approach to an inductive, historical and experiential approach to revelation, faith and theology (DV, 8 and 14;*GS*,4-5)
- a recommendation that a reading of the signs of the time should inform the presentation of the Gospel if the Church is to continue the mission of Christ in the world today (*GS*,4, 44; UR,4)
- a new awareness of anthropology as central to the proclamation of the Gospel (*GS*,3).

Alongside these generic changes, the following particular 'principles' were adopted which have a direct bearing on the conduct of Catholic education:

- a recognition by John XXIII that the substance of the ancient doctrine of the deposit of faith is one thing and the way it is presented is another[6]

---

6. John XXIII, 'Opening speech to the Council', *The Documents of Vatican II*, ed. by W. M. Abbott, London: Chapman, 1967: 710-719 at 715.

- an acknowledgement that the Church in its early history learned to adapt the Christian message to the concepts and languages of different people and that 'this kind of adaptation must ever be the law of all evangelisation' (GS, 44; AG, 22)
- an explicit awareness that an intimate relationship exists between faith and culture (GS, 57-58)
- when doctrines are being compared, in ecumenical dialogue, theologians should remember that 'in Catholic doctrine there exists an order or hierarchy of truths' which 'vary in the relation to the foundations of Christian faith' (UR, 11).

These theological shifts and educational principles within the overall vision of Vatican II, when taken together, mark a significant change in the self-understanding of Catholicism. They signal a development in the understanding of Catholic identity and how this should be communicated in Catholic education today. For many this development represents a paradigm shift. This change is often described as a movement out of a Christendom paradigm to a new paradigm of a Church in dialogue with the world.[7]

At Vatican II we encounter a Church no longer existing in opposition to or suspicion of the modern world, a Church reaching out in dialogue to other churches, a Church extending the hand of friendship to other religions, a Church committed to a process of teaching *and* learning in a new relationship of mutuality with the modern world (GS, 44).

---

7. See James E. McEvoy, *Leaving Christendom for Good: Church-World Dialogue in a Secular Age*, Maryland: Lexington books/Rowman and Littlefield, 2014.

These particular perspectives are no longer optional extras; they enter into the very definition of what it means to be Catholic in the contemporary world. Catholic identity is now made up of a finely tuned, dynamic relationship between *ressourcement* (going back to the sources) and continuous *aggiornamento* (updating).

c. *Declaration on Christian Education* (1965)

We are now in a position to approach the particular *Declaration on Christian Education* from the Council promulgated in October 1965, with 2,290 votes in favour and 35 against. This declaration was originally entitled the 'Catholic school' and subsequently changed to the much broader concept of 'Christian education'. The following is a schematic summary of the *Declaration* which does not claim to do it full justice:

- Christian education is a holistic praxis: concerned with the whole of human life, even the secular part of it in so far as it has a bearing on a heavenly calling (Introduction)
- True education 'aims at the formation of the human person in the pursuit of his/her ultimate end and of the good of society' (1)
- Christian education should be informed by 'the latest advances in psychology and the arts, and the science of teaching', seeking to promote the physical, moral and intellectual development of the person in the service of freedom and the common good (1)

- Christian formation should come up to the same standards as those obtaining in secular subjects (7)
- the goal of Christian education is the maturity of the human person as a child of God, conscious of the gift of faith, learning how to worship God, and understanding Christ as Redeemer (2)
- parents are the primary educators of children and it is in the family that children are taught to know and worship God, and to love the neighbour (3)
- parents should be 'free to choose according to their conscience the schools they want for their children' (6)
- Catholic schools, which can take on different forms, should be animated by the Gospel spirit of freedom and charity, open to the contemporary world, receptive of students who are not Catholic, and 'caring for ... those who are poor' (8 and 9)
- Catholic colleges and universities should promote harmony between faith and science as well as a convergence between faith and reason, and have a faculty of theology where possible (10 and 8).
- in non-Catholic universities there should be 'centres under Catholic auspices' (10).

Commentaries on the *Declaration on Christian Education* are few enough and are often more critical than positive.[8] According to Professor Joseph Ratzinger writing in 1966 'the text was not treated by the Council fathers with any

8. A positive reading of the *Declaration on Christian Education* and its implications can be found in Michael Drumm, 'The Extremely Important Issue of Education', *Vatican II in Ireland, Fifty Years On: Essays in Honour of Padraic Conway*, edited by Dermot A. Lane, Bern: Peter Lang, 2015: 285-303.

specific affection', partly because the council members were tiring as they moved towards a conclusion in December 1965.[9] Ratzinger saw the Declaration as 'unfortunately, a rather weak document'.[10] The US historian John O'Malley observes that the 'the document never entered centre stage at the Council'.[11] According to a contemporary commentator the Declaration failed 'to develop all of the possibilities of education implied by the anthropology of the Council'.[12] A further weakness is that 'it did not apply … .the council's larger reflection on the relationship of the church to the modern world'.[13] In spite of these criticisms, the full significance of the Declaration is to be found not in the text itself but in the many documents that the Congregation for Catholic education has issued in the last fifty years such as, to cite just three examples: *The Catholic School* (1977), *The Religious Dimension of Education in a Catholic School* (1988) and *Educating to Intercultural Dialogue in the Catholic School* (2013). The Declaration, like many other documents of Vatican II, marked a beginning and not an end.

---

9. Joseph Ratzinger, *Theological Highlights of Vatican II*, 179.

10. *Ibid*, 254.

11. John O'Malley, *What happened at Vatican II?*

12. Don J. Briel, 'The Declaration on Christian Education, GE', *Vatican II: Renewal within Tradition*, ed. by Mathew Lamb and M. Levering, New York: OUP, 2008: 383-396 at 389.

13. Ibid, 394.

PART TWO
A SOCIAL AND
CULTURAL ANALYSIS

a. Importance of Reading the Signs of the Times According to Vatican II

We can now apply some of the above theological shifts and educational principles to Catholic education in the twenty-first century. By far the most challenging shift is the Church's dialogical relationship with the modern world. To engage meaningfully in this dialogue, the Council charged the Church with the responsibility of reading the signs of the times and interpreting them in the light of the Gospel. (*GS*, 4 and 44)

The purpose of reading the signs of the times is to enable the Church to continue the mission of Christ in the world today and ensure that the Church is 'able to answer the ever recurring questions which people ask about the meaning of the present life and of the life to come' and 'to be aware of and understand the aspirations, the yearnings and often the dramatic features of the world in which we live' (*GS*, 3 and 4). Reading the signs of the times also enables the Church to implement the educational principle of adapting the proclamation of the Gospel to the language and culture of our age.

A further theological reason for reading the signs of the times is that history is the place where God acts in the world. Since God chose to reveal God's self in history, especially in the history of Israel and uniquely in the historical life of Jesus, then the Church must continue to discern how God is active in the world today.

A third reason, this time pneumatological, for reading the signs of the times is the recognition by the Church that 'the Spirit of God ... directs the course of time and renews the face of the earth' (*GS*, 26) and that humanity 'is continually being stimulated by the Spirit of God' (GS, 41). Reading the signs of the times is a first step in the process of enabling the Church to discern the action of the Spirit in the world. If this is the case, then the modern world should not be regarded as a place from which God is absent. Demonising the secular world is not the right educational direction for the Church to take. The secular world is a graced reality, a sacred place, and a holy space where we can find God if we look hard enough. Teilhard de Chardin, in the light of his scientific understanding of the universe, liked to point out that 'in virtue of the creation, and still more, of the Incarnation, nothing here below is profane to those who know how to see'.[14] Of course there are voices fiercely opposed to faith and religion, but these voices must be heard because often they have something of value to say to the type of faith and religion we represent.

b. A Plurality of Readings of the Signs of the Times

Given the importance of reading the signs of the times for the mission of the Church in the world and its credible proclamation of the Gospel, it is imperative to map out the social and cultural context in which Catholic education takes place today. There is, of course, a great variety of readings of the signs of the times.

For example, Lieven Boeve, the Belgian theologian, claims that European culture is characterised by secularisation, individualisation and de-traditionalisation. We are now living in a post-Christian and post-secular world where religion is

---

14. Teilhard de Chardin, *The Divine Millieu*, New York: Harper and Row, 1960: 64-65.

one item among others competing for attention in a world dominated by the influence of the media and market.[15]

Another not dis-similar reading can be found in the French Jesuit theologian Christoph Theobald. Theobald talks about the rapid rise of individualism alongside a diminishing confidence in all social institutions. The grand narratives of meaning are collapsing and people are left 'to their own devices ... to find their own ways' tossed as they are between 'the different models that the powerful put forward in advertising and their personal desire for something creative'.[16] Quoting Marcel Gauchet, he suggests: 'We are doomed from henceforth to live in nakedness and anguish ... something from which we were spared up to now by the good offices of the gods'.[17] A further point emphasised by Theobald is that in our postmodern society we are losing our capacity for concentration which is essential to creativity. This last point is a feature not only of secular society but also within the contemporary Church.

c. Signs of the Times According to Charles Taylor

However, in spite of the obvious value of these readings, I want to focus on Charles Taylor's social and cultural analysis of the world in which we live today.[18] I find Taylor's analysis

15. Lieven Boeve, *God Interrupts History: Theology in a Time of Upheaval*, New York: Continuum, 2007: 13-29.

16. Christoph Theobald, 'An Ignatian Way of Doing Theology: Theology through discerning The True Life', *The Way*, 43/4, October 2004: 146-160 at 155 and 166.

17. Ibid, 155.

18. Charles Taylor, *A Secular Age*, Harvard University Press, 2007.

most pertinent to the challenges facing Catholic education in the twenty-first century, especially his outline of the gradual shift over a period of five hundred years from a situation of belief to widespread unbelief in the twentieth century and his association of this drift with anthropology. Though this shift happened in Ireland only in the last thirty or forty years, Taylor's analysis can enlighten our understanding of the Irish experience of the dramatic movement from belief to unbelief in the late twentieth century.

Since Taylor takes eight hundred pages to map out this journey from belief to unbelief we can only outline the key moments in this shift. Taylor, in *A Secular Age* (2007) charts the decline of belief in which we have moved from a situation in which faith was the norm to a new situation in which unbelief is the new norm for an ever increasing number of people. This did not happen over night, but took place gradually under the weight of the enlightenment, the rise of modernity, and the emerging processes of secularisation. For Taylor there arose what he calls the emergence of a purely 'immanent frame' of reference, the rise of an 'exclusive humanism', and the development of a 'disenchanted universe', all devoid of any external reference to Transcendence.

These developments in turn shaped what Taylor terms the 'modern social imaginary'. This new social imaginary is not just another theory about society, but rather what he describes as 'the generally shared background understandings of society, which make it possible for it to function', that is, 'ways in which people imagine their social existence, how they fit together with others, how things go on between them and their fellows.'[19]

---

19. Op. cit., 323.

Further, this social imaginary is accompanied by a cosmic imaginary, which is 'impersonal in the most forbidding sense, blind and indifferent to our fate'.[20] For Taylor, 'what is unprecedented in human history is (that) there is no longer a clear and obvious sense in which this vastness is shaped and limited by an antecedent plan'.[21] Taylor sums up: 'everyone can agree the big difference between us and our ancestors of five hundred years ago is that they lived in an enchanted world and we do not'.[22]

All of this begs the following questions: when did this happen in Ireland? What was the tipping point? How did this shift take place socially and culturally? In response to these questions, Taylor makes a distinctive contribution to reading of the signs of the times, a reading that is of singular importance to the challenges facing Catholic education in the twenty-first century. For Taylor, one of the most influential factors facilitating this shift from belief to unbelief is anthropology. It should be remembered that Taylor gave an extensive analysis of anthropology in *Sources of the Self: The Making of Modern Identity* (1989) that influenced his writing of *A Secular Age* (2007).

d. Taylor's Focus on Anthropology

In his account of anthropology, Taylor introduces a fundamental distinction between what he calls the pre-

20. Op.cit., 363.

21. 325.

22. C. Taylor, 'Western Secularity', *Rethinking Secularism,* ed. by Craig Calhoun, M. Juergensmeyer and J. VanAntwerpen, New York: OUP, 2011:38.

modern 'porous self' (open self) and modern 'buffered self' (enclosed self). The porous self, going back to the medieval world, is open to spirits, demons and other cosmic forces not under our control. The porous self is an engaged self, involved seamlessly in the natural and supernatural worlds.

In contrast, the buffered self of the modern era is an enclosed self who sets up a boundary, a wall, as it were, between the self and the world, between the mind and the body. The buffered self is disengaged from the natural and supernatural worlds, dis-embedded from society, and disenchanted with the universe. The buffered self closes itself off from any transcendental horizon and lives life solely within an immanent frame. A sharp contrast and dualism emerges between the natural world and the supernatural world, between the immanent frame of reference and the possibility of a transcendent point of reference. This process of disengagement from the natural/supernatural world, the dis-embedding of the self from society, and the disenchantment of the self from the universe poses serious challenges for the formation of human identity and in particular for Catholic identity which builds on human identity.

One of the many factors facilitating this turning towards an exclusively immanent frame of reference was the rise of Deism in the late seventeenth century and throughout the eighteenth century, an image of God without any ongoing personal relationship with the world. This Deism placed great emphasis on the importance of establishing a moral order which in turn fuelled the development of an exclusive humanism and a corresponding decline of faith in a personal God.

To complete this account of anthropology we need to move beyond Taylor to say something about the postmodern critique of the self. Not all is well with the buffered self of modernity. A strong reaction to and critique of the modern self has been offered by the culture of post-modernity. For some, the self, whether porous or buffered, is merely a rhetorical flourish, something of a linguistic and cultural device, to facilitate the interaction of differences. For others the self is just a convenient site for the transactions of power and desire. This site, however, has no unified ground or enduring existence. Note once again the issue of human identity arises. Richard Rorty sums up this position when he says about the self: 'there is nothing deep down inside except what we have put there ourselves'.[23]

e. Anthropology – An Emerging Challenge for Education and Theology

It is surely obvious that anthropology plays a pivotal role in the shift from belief to unbelief. The movement from the open, porous self to the closed, buffered self and now from the buffered self to the deconstructed self of postmodernity is of enormous significance for Catholic education and theology. It is no exaggeration to say that the contemporary self is in crisis and in need of rehabilitation. Evidence of this crisis can be found in a variety of places: in gender studies; in ecology; in ethics; in biomedical sciences; in faith formation; and in the God question to mention but a few.

---

23. Richard Rorty, *Consequences of Pragmatism*, Minnesota: University of Minnesota Press, 1982: xliii.

Vivid expressions of this crisis can be found in a questioning going on in the arts around the self and human identity. Films such as *Amour* (2012), directed by Michael Haneke, address head on the anthropological conundrums of age, failure and disintegration in the lives of an elderly couple, one of whom has suffered a stroke. This movie provoked one reviewer to invoke, by way of response to the question, the unexpected line in Philip Larkin's poem, 'An Arundel Tomb': 'what will survive of us is love.' Another movie, *Still Alice* (2014), directed by Richard Glatzer and Wash Westmoreland deals with the early-onset Alzheimer's disease in the life of a professor of linguistics just after her fiftieth birthday. The film has been described as a moving meditation on who we really are and raises questions about what happens to the core identity of Alice as a result of the onset of Alzheimer's. And a third film, *The Theory of Everything*, about the life of Stephen Hawking, portrays graphically a searching preoccupation with self. Similarly Tom Stoppard's 2015 play, *The Hard Problem*, struggles with the question whether consciousness is merely a physical function of the brain or a separate experience designated by words like mind, or soul, or conscience, or spirit.

If, as we have seen, Christian education is about the holistic development of the human, the formation of the person and the development of a particular identity, then anthropology is key. Awareness of this importance can be found in the working document drawn up by the Congregation for Catholic Education entitled, *Educating Today and Tomorrow: A Renewing Passion* (2014). This is a discussion document, known as the *Instrumentum Laboris*, put together in preparation for the fiftieth anniversary of the

Declaration in November 2015. Under the heading 'Current and future Educational Challenges' there is a paragraph devoted to anthropology which is worth quoting in full:

'First of all we must express the anthropology underlining our educational vision for the twenty-first century in *different* terms:
  - it is a philosophical anthropology that must also be an anthropology of truth, that is a social anthropology whereby man is seen in his relationship and way of being
  - an anthropology of recollection and promise
  - an anthropology that refers to the cosmos and cares about sustainable development
  - and even more an anthropology that refers to God.

The gaze of faith and hope, which is its foundation, looks at reality to discover God's plan. Thus, starting from a profound reflection on modern man and the contemporary world, we must *redefine our vision* regarding education.' (Chapter 3, paragraph 6, italics added).

This working document makes an insightful diagnosis, especially in chapter 3, and in particular paragraph 6, of the challenges facing Catholic education in the twenty-first century.

We see that the arts and the *Instrumentum Laboris* for the celebration of the fiftieth anniversary of the Declaration in their own distinctive ways go to the heart of the problem facing Catholic education today. They show an awareness that anthropology is in crisis, in need of reconstruction and rehabilitation. Anthropology has always been important in Catholic theology and appears throughout the Christian narrative in terms of creation and the fall, sin and redemption, nature and grace, faith and freedom. However, something new is taking place here. Anthropology, in itself, is emerging as a *locus theologicus* and therefore belongs to the centre of Catholic education and theology.

Anthropology was central in the renewal of Catholic theology in the twentieth century that preceded Vatican II in the writings of Karl Rahner, Bernard Lonergan and Edward Schillebeeck. The importance of anthropology in itself is recognised for the first time in *Gaudium et Spes* at the Council, more recently in *Instrumentum Laboris* (2014) and in *Laudato Si'*, as we shall see in Part 3 below. Water Kasper talks explicitly about 'an anthropological turn' at Vatican II.[24] This turn to anthropology was also recognised by the young Professor Ratzinger as legitimate even though he had some misgivings about it.[25]

f. A Note on Rahner's Influential Anthropology

Before examining *Gaudium et Spes* on anthropology, it will be illuminating to summarise Karl Rahner's theological anthropology by way of background to what happened at Vatican II. From early on, Rahner presented the human person as a potential 'Hearer of the Word'. The human is a dynamic, restless, self-transcending being orientated towards mystery and therefore open to hearing a word from God. For Rahner, the human is an always-already-graced

---

24. Water Kasper, 'The theological anthropology of *Gaudium et Spes*', *Communio* 23, 1996:129-140 at 130-131.

25. See footnote 30 below.

being, and so, therefore, finding God is not about discovering something new. Instead, discovering God is about entering more fully into that with which we are already familiar, however vague or ill-defined that familiarity may be in terms of the dynamic intentionality of human consciousness, the still voice of conscience, the restlessness of human spirit, or the yearnings of the soul. For Rahner, anthropology leads to theology and so he writes that 'dogmatic theology today must be theological anthropology'.[26]

Secondly, because the human is the site of God's self-communication to the world, there is a close link between anthropology and Christology. Back in 1954, well before the council, Rahner was suggesting 'that Christology may be studied as a self-transcending anthropology, and anthropology as a deficient Christology.'[27] Later, Rahner elaborated on this by stating that 'Christology is the end and the beginning of anthropology'.[28]

Thirdly, Rahner posited a close relationship between anthropology and eschatology. He saw eschatology as anthropology conjugated in the future tense on the basis of what happened in the life of Jesus.[29] Eschatology is about the completion, fulfilment and transformation of anthropology. In effect, Rahner's anthropology is played out in his theology of grace, Christology and eschatology. These views of Rahner turned out to be influential at the Council.

---

26. Karl Rahner, 'Anthropology and Theology', *Theological Investigations*, vol. 9, Writings of 1965-7, London, 1972, 28 and 34.

27. Karl Rahner, 'Current Problems in Christology', *Theological Investigations*, vol. 1, 149-200 at 164 footnote 1.

28. Rahner, 'Theology of the Incarnation', *Theological Investigations*, vol. 4, 117.

29. 'Theology and Anthropology': *Theological Investigations*, vol 9, 45 and *Foundations of the Christian Faith*, London, 1978, 431.

In retrospect it might be said that Rahner's transcendental anthropology was insufficiently rooted in the vagaries of history and his theology perhaps too anthropocentric given the current ecological crisis. In light of the above structural changes and educational principles, Taylor's anthropological reading of the signs of the times, and the post-modern critique of the self, it is time to look at the anthropology of the Second Vatican Council as expressed in *Gaudium et Spes*.

g. The Anthropology of *Gaudium et Spes*

That *Gaudium et Spes* embodied an anthropological turn is beyond question. Ratzinger captures succinctly the novelty of this development at the Council. He points out that *Gaudium et Spes* 'dares to present theology as an anthropology and only becomes radically theological by including man in the discourse about God by way of Christ, thus manifesting the deepest unity of theology'.[30] What is distinctive about *Gaudium et Spes* is not so much its adoption of anthropology as a point of departure, but that the anthropology proposed is a Christological anthropology: 'Christology is ... the criterion of all its statements about anthropology'.[31] In broad terms, the first three chapters contain an anthropological vision.

Gaudium et Spes begins by pointing out that 'the focal point of our total presentation is man himself, whole and entire, body and soul, heart and conscience, mind and will.' and then goes on to say that 'according to the almost unanimous

---

30. Joseph Ratzinger, 'Pastoral Constitution on the Church in the Modern World' *Commentary on the Documents of Vatican II*, ed. by Herbert Vorgrimler, vol. 5, New York: Herder and Herder, 1969: 159 and also 117-118.

31. Walter Kasper, *art. cit.*137.

opinion of believers and unbelievers alike, all things on the earth should be related to the human as to their centre and crown' (12). Here the council is trying to find an anthropology that would be acceptable to all, but in doing so has lapsed into an anthropocentrism that ecologists today would not accept.

In article 4, it points out 'the human race is involved in a new stage of history' in which significant 'social and cultural transformations' have taken place. These changes, in turn have repercussions on the religious life of individuals. In the midst of all the advances of the modern world, the individual, nonetheless, 'frequently appears more unsure' and is often 'paralysed by uncertainty'(4). Further, in spite of all the progress, the modern world is full of contradictions, made up of power and weakness, noble and foul deeds, freedom and slavery (9).

Gaudium et Spes adopts an overly optimistic view of the human's cognitive capacity, claiming, for example, that the individual 'shares in the light of the divine mind' and so 'can with genuine certitude attain to reality itself as knowable', even though it admits, as a result of sin 'that certitude is partly obscured and weakened' (15).

Gaudium et Spes explores the mortality of the human, pointing out that the individual is 'tormented by pain' by 'the advancing deterioration of his body', and by a 'dread of perpetual extinction' (18). Consequently, the human 'rebels against death because the human bears ... an eternal seed which cannot be reduced to matter' (18). In the face of these issues troubling humanity, *Gaudium et Spes* points out that 'God has called the human ... to an endless sharing of divine life beyond all corruption and that Christ has made this possible by his historical death and resurrection' (18).

This Christological response to the anguish of humanity is spelled out explicitly in article 22 which has a number of key statements, drawing on Christology as the criterion of anthropology:

- 'Only in the mystery of the Word incarnate does the mystery of the human take on light' because 'Christ, the final Adam, by the revelation of the mystery of the Father ... fully reveals man to man himself and makes his supreme calling clear'
- Christ 'who is the image of the invisible God is himself perfect man' who restores the divine likeness which had been disfigured from the first sin onwards
- by the Incarnation, the Son of God has united God's self in some fashion with every human being.

This rich Christological article of *Gaudium et Spes* presents Christ as the revelation of the human, that is the exemplar of what it means to be human, and at the same time sees Christ as the revelation of the Father to the world. In this article, the Council adopts a theological, Christological and eschatological anthropology as normative. This normative character of Christology is revealed in a variety of ways throughout *Gaudium et Spes*. For example, *Gaudium et Spes* presents Christ as 'the goal of history, the focal point of the desires of history and civilisation, the centre of humanity, the joy of all hearts, and the fulfilment of all aspirations' (45 and 10).

A further underlying theme in *Gaudium et Spes* is the social character of the human. God, it points out, 'did not create the human as a solitary' (12). Instead, God created male and female, and their companionship 'produces the primary form of interpersonal communion'. And then it goes on to say 'by her/his innermost nature the human is a social being' (12). Later, *Gaudium et Spes* expands this social understanding of the human further: the human 'cannot fully find himself/herself except through a sincere gift of herself/himself' – a point that anticipates something of what Emmanuel Levinas, Paul Ricoeur, and Jean-Luc Marion have to say about anthropology.

The council explicitly affirms the dignity and equality of every human being and it also notes how this dignity and equality demands respect for difference: 'Respect and love ought to be extended ... to those who think or act differently than we do in social, political and even religious matters' (28). This dignity and equality is based on an understanding that every human being possesses a soul, is created in the image and likeness of God, is redeemed in Christ, and shares in a common destiny in God. Consequently, 'every type of discrimination ... based on sex, race, colour, social condition, language or religion' is contrary to God's will (29). This vision is still awaiting ecclesial and pastoral implementation. These theological, Christological and eschatological perspectives on what it means to be human provides a context at least for discussing the questions raised by the above movies and the play by Tom Stoppard.

h. Evaluation of the Anthropology of *Gaudium et Spes*

There is much of enduring value in *Gaudium et Spes*: the turn to anthropology, the emphasis on the social dimension of the person, the dignity and equality of all human beings, the presentation of Christ as the exemplar of what it means to be fully human, the adoption of a kenotic anthropology, and the critical embrace of the modern world.

Perhaps more important from the point of view of Catholic education is the methodology of *Gaudium et Spes* in reading the signs of the times which informs the law of adaptation in the service of the gospel. Equally challenging is the appreciation by *Gaudium et Spes* of the necessary relationship between faith and culture, and the need for faith to engage critically and creatively with contemporary culture.

For Paul VI the split between faith and culture was described as the drama of our time.[32] Likewise, John Paul II sought energetically to enculturate the gospel message, pointing out that a faith that is not enculturated is not a living faith. The French theologian Henry Gagey suggests that the 'exculturation' of the ecclesial message from contemporary culture is the source of alienation for many in the Church today.[33] This disconnect between faith and contemporary culture is the greatest challenge facing Catholic education today. The Church no longer seems to have the language to engage with culture, and yet language, as we shall presently see, is an essential element in the constitution of the human. What is of lasting value from *Gaudium et Spes* is the recognition of the importance of dialogue: within the Church, within culture, with the other churches, with other religions, and with atheism (92).

32. Paul VI, *Evangelii Nuntiandi*, 1975, 20.

33. Henri-Jerome Gagey, 'La dimension ecclesiale de la foi aujourd hui', *Rescherches de science religieuse*, 2012/4: 485-504.

In praising *Gaudium et Spes*, we must also acknowledge its limitations. It should be noted that just as the Catholic Church was embracing the modern world, others were moving away from modernity and this is even more so the case today some fifty years on.[34] This does not mean reverting to a pre-modern world as some would have it. Instead, we must move forward creatively within the crucible of modernity, critically conscious of its strengths and weaknesses. There is no way around the crucible of the many modernities of contemporary culture.

Secondly we must acknowledge, as Rahner and Ratzinger did during the Council, that the outlook of *Gaudium et Spes* is too optimistic and progressivist, with insufficient attention given to the cross. And yet, it must be acknowledged that the document does have scattered references to a theology of the Paschal mystery awaiting elaboration (eg, 22, 37, 38).

A third limitation is the presence within *Gaudium et Spes* of traces of anthropocentrism which needs to be critiqued, especially in the light of the new encyclical.[35] Further, there is an inflated confidence in the capacity of the human to know reality, a view that has come in for severe criticism from proponents of postmodernity. The all-knowing subject of modernity has been found to be wanting on a number of fronts: neglect of otherness, especially marginalised others, and neglect of historical developments in hermeneutics

---

34. Lieven Boeve,'*Gaudium et Spes* and the Crisis of Modernity: The End of Dialogue with the World?' *Vatican II and Its Legacy*, ed. by M. Lamberigts and L. Kenis, Leuven University Press, 2002:83-94.

35. See the helpful and influential article by Denis Edwards, 'Anthropocentrism and its Ecological Critique: A Theological response', *Being Buman: Groundwork for a theological anthropology for the 21st century*, ed.by David Kirchhoffer with R. Horner and P. Mc Ardle, Oregon: Wipf and Stock, 2013: 107-121.

which highlight the influence of place and culture in knowing. Far greater humility is required of the Church concerning what it knows and does not know from revelation.

Perhaps the most balanced evaluation of *Gaudium et Spes* is given by Ormond Rush who points to a variety of ambiguities and tensions at the Council, especially in *Gaudium et Spes*, many of which are still felt in the Church today:

- tensions between a sociological and theological approach to questions of the day
- between a deductive and inductive methodology
- between anthropology and Christology as a point of departure
- between Christology and Pneumatology
- between a Thomist and an Augustinian vision of the human
- between an optimistic outlook and a pessimistic view of the world
- between the classical view of the human and a historical view
- between an extrinsic model and intrinsic model of God's action in history.[36]

---

36. Ormond Rush, 'Unresolved tensions within *Gaudium et Spes*: Agenda for a contemporary Anthropology', *Being Human*, 35-46.

PART THREE
THE IMPLICATIONS OF *LAUDATO SI'* FOR EDUCATION

a. Introduction to a Far-Reaching Multifaceted Encyclical

The publication of *Laudato Si'* in 2015 coincides with the fiftieth anniversary of the closure of the Second Vatican Council. The encyclical applies many of the insights of the Council, especially those of *Gaudium et Spes*. This new encyclical addresses the ecological crisis of the twenty-first century by drawing on and adding to the rich tradition of Catholic Social Teaching and the structural shifts of Vatican II discussed above.

Laudato Si' calls for nothing less than a 'bold cultural revolution' (114) and a profound ecological conversion.

The encyclical examines the current ecological crisis at a number of different levels: from the science of climate change, to a critique of economic models, to an outline of the vision of the Gospel, to a review of technology, to the importance of a call to action, and to the need for an ecological spirituality. It is a far-reaching, complex document. Here we will limit ourselves to some of the more immediate implications of the encyclical for Catholic education.

There are at least three areas in the encyclical that are related directly to the challenges facing Catholic education in the twenty-first century. These are the encyclical's critique of anthropocentrism, its outline of what it calls 'the educational challenge' demanded by the encyclical, and the call for 'ecological conversion'. These three areas have a bearing on the conduct of Catholic religious education and theology in the twenty-first century.[37]

---

37. A helpful introduction to the encyclical can be found in Donal Dorr, 'The Ecology Encyclical', *The Furrow*, 2015, 387-393.

b. The Critique in *Laudato Si'* of Anthropocentrism

One of the underlying themes within the encyclical, sometimes explicit, and at other times implicit, is anthropology. Francis is very clear that 'many things have to change course, but it is we human beings above all who need to change. We lack an awareness of our common origin, of our mutual belonging, of a future to be shared with everyone' (202). No amount of education will succeed unless and until we come up with 'a new way of thinking about human beings' (215). The modern self-understanding of man is a major part of the ecological crisis: 'There can be no ecology without an adequate anthropology' (118).

This encyclical puts up in neon lights what it calls, in a heading in chapter three, 'The Crisis and Effects of Modern Anthropocentrism'. The encyclical rails against what it names as 'tyrannical' (68), 'distorted' (69), and 'misguided' (118, 119, 122) anthropocentrism. These are strong adjectives and they leave no room for ambiguity. In particular, the encyclical points out that 'modernity has been marked by an excessive anthropocentrism' and this has compromised the intrinsic dignity of the natural world (115). Note the causal connection being made between the self-understanding of modern man and the damaged dignity of the natural world. It is increasingly clear that climate change is caused by human beings. Francis goes further by stating: 'Once the human being declares independence from reality and behaves with absolute dominion, the very foundations of culture begin to crumble'. When this happens, 'man sets himself up in the place of God and ends up provoking a rebellion on the part of nature'(117).

There are a number of charges here. The encyclical argues that there is a causal connection between the behaviour of human beings and the ecological crisis brought about by climate change. Further, the encyclical talks about the reaction, the 'rebellion', of nature to this behaviour of human beings. Moreover, the encyclical notes how humans have presumed to take the place of the divine. These forms of anthropocentrism need to be critiqued and replaced by a new anthropology. A more chastened and humbled anthropology is necessary to respond to the ecological crisis of the twenty-first century.

The encyclical acknowledges that an 'inadequate presentation of Christian anthropology gave rise to a wrong understanding of the relationship between human beings and the world'. What 'was handed on was a Promethean vision of mastery over the world' and this gave 'the impression that the protection of nature was something that only the faint-hearted cared about'. The call to 'dominion', contrary to popular perception, is a call to 'responsible stewardship' and not exploitation (116).

The human, therefore, needs to be de-centred in order to be re-connected within a larger scheme of things. The ecological crisis is both an anthropological crisis and a theological crisis. Anthropology is one of the sources of the ecological crisis as well as one of the solutions to this crisis.

c. Educational Challenges of the Encyclical

It is more than a coincidence that the concluding chapter of the encyclical is given over to the 'Ecological Education and Spirituality'. This chapter begins by noting that 'many things have to change but it is we human beings above all who need to change' (202). The encyclical deals in a number of places with the 'educational challenge' facing humanity at this time (202 and 209). This educational challenge arises, in part, out of a lack of awareness on several different, but related, areas. There is a lack of awareness concerning 'our common origins', 'our mutual belonging' to each other, and 'a future to be shared with everyone' (202). This seemingly small sentence contains a big educational agenda around origins, human belonging and a shared future.

Cosmology and biological evolution would be a good place to begin in addressing our common origins: the new cosmic story, the recent arrival of humans within cosmic history and the organic unity of the universe. These findings give us a new sense of the place of the human within a larger picture. The question of mutual belonging is explicitly an anthropological issue, highlighting the mutuality, inter-relatedness, and interdependence of human beings. Human beings need each other and cannot survive without each other or without remaining interconnected. The issues of 'a future to be shared' raise important questions about justice between the nations, justice between the generations, the existence of an ecological debt between the global North and South, as well as eschatological issues around the future of creation, humanity and history.

An important part of the educational challenge is to go beyond 'the compulsive consumerism' (203) promoted by the free market. This consumerism gives people an impression that they are free because 'they have ... the freedom to consume' (203) when, in reality, such consumerism restricts freedom to an endless repetition of the same, limits the horizons of choice, and eliminates the possibility of hope in the future. Linked to this confusion is the suggestion that 'postmodern humanity has not yet achieved a new self-awareness capable of offering guidance and direction'. This absence of awareness and this lack of a clear identity 'is a source of anxiety' (203) which in turn 'engenders a feeling of instability and uncertainty'. This uncertainty can cause people to 'become self-centred and self-enclosed' (204 and 208).

These issues are clearly anthropological, and reflect some of the issues we have already referred to above as the 'contemporary crisis of the modern self'. We have seen the need to move forward to a higher synthesis that brings together aspects of the pre-modern, modern and post-modern self. A new vision of what it means to be human is called for at this time (215). We will try to offer some pointers in relation to this new vision of what it means to be human in the concluding section of this paper.

In addition to these anthropological implications of the educational challenge, the encyclical also outlines some of the areas that need to be addressed in any programme of 'environmental education' (210). In recent times, the goals of ecological education have been broadened to go beyond scientific information, consciousness-raising, and the prevention of environmental risks. The encyclical proposes three particular goals for ecological education in the present: a critique of the myths of modernity grounded in a utilitarian mind-set, the restoration of various levels of ecological equilibrium, and a leap towards a transcendent ground for ecological ethics (210).

Each of these goals is a major educational programme. The encyclical simply hints at some broad outlines of what is entailed in each goal. Under the critique of the myths of modernity, it refers, in brackets, to a number of issues such as individualism, unlimited progress, competition, consumerism, the unregulated market. These subjects are addressed throughout the encyclical.

One of these goals is worth highlighting here, namely the modern myth of unlimited progress and growth. The encyclical boldly asserts that 'the idea of infinite or unlimited growth, which proves so attractive to economists, financiers, and experts in technology' is 'based on the lie that there is an infinite supply of the earth's goods' which 'leads to the planet being squeezed dry beyond every limit' (106). It is simply not true that there is 'an infinite quantity of energy and resources available' (106 and 78).

In criticising the myths of modernity, the encyclical is quite nuanced. On the one hand, it praises the advances of modernity, 'especially in the fields of medicine, engineering and communications' (107). On the other hand, it points out that 'our immense technological development has not been accompanied by a development in human responsibility, values and conscience' (105). *Laudato Si'* is, in effect, outlining how modernity and technology are part of the problem relating to climate change, poverty and inequality and, at the same time, are also a part of the solution in addressing these realities.

A second goal for education is the recovery of some form of ecological equilibrium within our lives. This means 'establishing harmony within ourselves, with others, with nature and other living creatures, and with God' (210). The encyclical is seeking to promote holistic education, pointing out almost as a mantra, that everything is inter-related, inter-connected and inter-dependent. This entails a recovery of the broken relationship that exists between humans, the earth and God (66). In particular, the encyclical highlights the gap that exists between the human and the natural world, between humans and the earth, which is largely responsible for the attitude of domination and exploitation of the earth's resources.

The third goal of ecological education is that of helping people to make 'the leap towards the transcendent which gives ecological ethics its deepest meaning' (210). Part of the challenge here is to develop an ethics of ecology that all can adopt in terms of a new solidarity with creation, a responsibility of all for the natural world, and a compassionate care of our common home. It should be borne in mind that the encyclical is 'an invitation to every person living on this planet ... to enter into dialogue with all people about our common home' (3). A shared ethic for all is imperative if we are to save the planet. On the other hand, there is the challenge to theology to provide a transcendent foundation for such a shared ethic. Having stated this goal for ecological education, it is striking that the encyclical concludes this section on education by stating that all of these efforts will be inadequate unless we can come up with 'new ways of thinking about human beings, life, society, and our relationship with nature' (215). The centre piece of ecological education and ethics is, therefore, anthropology.

d. The Call to Ecological Conversion

This brings us to the third theme of the encyclical that has a direct bearing on Catholic education in the twenty-first century, namely the call to ecological conversion. In light of this encyclical, ecological education becomes an intrinsic element within Catholic education. Further, an effective ecological education will lead to ecological conversion.

The encyclical deals with two forms of ecological conversion. On the one hand, it calls for a 'profound interior conversion' (217). At the centre of this conversion is an encounter with Christ which affects our relationship with the world around us. Being a Christian carries with it a commitment to protect God's creation, not as something optional but as 'essential to a life of virtue' (217). This task, the encyclical acknowledges, is too great on a purely individual level. Consequently, ecological conversion, if it is to bring about a lasting change, also requires 'a community conversion'. In other words, we can only succeed in saving the planet and protecting creation if we work together. Individual conversion needs the support of a community and the community depends on individuals. For this conversion, individual and communal, to succeed there is a need for 'a number of attitudes which foster a spirit of generous care' (220). These attitudes include:

- A sense of gratitude which recognises that the world is God's loving gift to us (220) and that, therefore, each moment is a gift from God to be lived to the full (226)
- A loving awareness that we are connected to other creatures and are a part of a universal communion (220)
- A recognition 'that each creature reflects something of God and has a message to convey to us' (221)

- An acceptance that 'Christ has taken unto himself this material world and, now risen, is present to each being ... penetrating it with his light' (221)
- A 'recognition that God created the world, writing into it an order and dynamism that human beings have no right to ignore' (221).

One of *Laudato Si*'s greatest strengths is the way it pinpoints modern anthropocentrism as one of the sources of the ecological crisis. The encyclical also calls for 'a new synthesis' in our understanding of the relationships between God, the human and the earth (121). This encyclical also invites a new reflection on the dignity of the natural world, the intrinsic relation between the natural order and human beings, and a recovery of an 'I-Thou' relationship between the earth, humanity and God (81 and 119). Further, the encyclical states clearly that ecological conversion is not something 'optional' or 'secondary'. Instead ecological conversion is intrinsic to Christian experience (217). Ecology enriches the identity of Christian faith and therefore must become a vital part of evangelisation.

In addition to the centrality of individual and communal conversion, the encyclical also talks about the importance of change in key areas of life such as politics, economics and business 'which should consider their environmental footprint and their patterns of production'(206).

PART FOUR
TOWARDS A RENEWED ANTHROPOLOGY

a. Challenges for Anthropology in the Twenty-First Century

We must now look, in the light of Vatican II and *Laudato Si'* at some of the anthropological challenges facing Catholic education and theology in the twenty-first century. The anthropological questions today are different to those of the latter half of the twentieth century as is clear in *Laudato Si'*. *Gaudium et Spes* has given principles, but not answers for the questions of the twenty-first century. And *Laudato Si'* has pointed a way forward.

As noted above, the premodern, modern, and postmodern self is in deep crisis today. The dignity of the person is assailed from many sides: pornography, consumerism, market capitalism, and globalisation. Questions around anthropology are myriad and include issues like radical individualism, the myth of the self-sufficient subject, the commodification of the self through market demands, the deconstruction of the self by postmodernity, gender issues, the spiritual and cultural isolation of the self in the twenty-first century.

In particular commentators like Richard Kearney point to a new alienation of the self from the flesh through the pervasive presence of technology.[38] Charles Taylor talks about 'excarnation' of the self from bodily form and the disengagement of reason from the flesh.[39] Others are concerned about the loss of existential inwardness, the neglect of human subjectivity, and the decline of interiority. One particular description of this can be found

---

38. Richard Kearney, 'Losing Our Touch', *New York Times*, 30 August 2014, Opinion subscription.

39. Charles Taylor, op. cit., 613.

in the 'reduction of the mind to software and the brain to a computer'.[40] To move in another direction and by way of conclusion to this paper we will outline some elements that might be used in the reconstruction of anthropology for the twenty-first century.

b. Elements in the Reconstruction of Anthropology

It is time to move beyond the premodern porous self, the buffered/enclosed self of modernity, and the elusive self of post-modernity. Strictly speaking, however, we cannot go *beyond* the premodern, modern and postmodern perceptions of the self. Instead we must go *through* these different anthropologies, retrieving what is of value, and move towards a higher synthesis of what it means to be human in the twenty-first century. For example, pre-modern anthropologies had a strong sense of belonging to a larger whole, in which the human, nature and the Creator were closely interconnected. There is a value in retrieving this organic perspective in a world that has become fragmented, fractured and increasingly scattered. Likewise, modern anthropology had a keen awareness of the importance of the individual, though at times this had become overblown, totalising and dominating vis-a-vis the other. Nonetheless there is an important insight here about the uniqueness and dignity of every individual that should not be lost in the search for the human in the twenty-first century. Similarly,

40. Jackson Lears, 'A place and time apart: the liberal arts vs neoliberalism' (review article on W. Deresiewicz, *The Excellent Sheep: The Mis-education of the American elite and the way to a Meaningful life*, 2014), Commonweal, 1 May 2015:14-21 at 16.

post-modern perspectives point to the instability of the self and its fragile character. Vulnerability and contingency, in contrast to the alleged autonomy of modernity, are characteristics of the post-modern self, aspects of the self that sharpen the search for salvation in a world that seems empty and vacant at times. It is, therefore, urgent to begin to recover the intrinsic, organic relationship between God, the self and the cosmos as recommended by *Laudato Si'*.

One of the refrains throughout *Laudato Si'* is that we are all interconnected (16, 42, 240). For Francis, 'the world, created according to a divine model ... is a web of relations' (240). Everything in the world is interconnected (16, 91, 240) and interrelated (91, 92, 120, 137, 141 and 142), and 'interdependent' (164). According to Francis, 'it is proper to every living being to tend towards other things, so that throughout the universe we can find any number of constant and secretly interwoven relationships' (240) – a view that stands out in stark contrast to the individualism and self-sufficiency of modernity. In the same article, Francis, echoing *Gaudium et Spes* (24), points out that the 'person grows more, matures more and is sanctified more to the extent that he or she enters into relationships, going out from themselves to live in communion with God, with others and with all creatures' (240). Here Pope Francis is doing two things. First of all, he is pointing towards a self-emptying, paschal anthropology based on the Paschal Mystery of Christ. Secondly, he is seeking to retrieve the spirit of the Middle Ages that assumed an integrated relationship between God, the self and the cosmos.

What is now needed is a plurality of anthropologies in the service of Catholic education and not just one model of what it means to be human because we live in and out of a plurality of identities. The following represents some building blocks for the reconstruction of a plurality of anthropologies in the twenty-first century.

c. The Human as Relational, Dialogical, Embodied, Linguistic, and No Longer Living in an Anthropocentric Universe

Relationality. In the first instance, pride of place must be given to the primacy of relationality in the reconstruction of what it means to be human. This means in effect we must move beyond the enduring influence of René Descartes (1596-1650) towards an anthropology which recognises first of all that 'we are, before I am', or, as an African proverb puts it 'we relate, therefore I am'. According to Teilhard de Chardin, reflecting on evolution, 'what comes first in the world for our thought is not "being" but "union" which produces this being'.[41] It is union that differentiates. In effect, being is first a 'we' before it can become an 'I'.[42] Relationality comes before individuality. The premodern porous self is not only historically prior but also ontologically prior to the modern buffered self. To exist, therefore, is always to coexist and to be is to be in relation. Evidence for this emphasis on the primacy of relationality can be found in the fact that we come into the world in a condition of dependent relationality and more often than not we leave the world in a similar state.

41. De Chardin, *Christianity and Evolution*, London: Collins, 1971: 227.

42. Ilia Delio, 'Evolution and the rise of the secular God', *From Teilhard to Omega: Co-creators in an Unfinished Universe*, New York: Orbis books, 2014: 42-43.

This emphasis on relationality should not be construed as a denial of the importance of individuality or the uniqueness of every human being, but rather a recovery of the matrix in which the self comes into being and begins to exist historically. Instead of moving from individualism to relationality which is the common perception, we must begin with a union that differentiates. We do not come into the world with a ready-made self; instead we leave the world with a self emerging as an unfinished work, as a work-in-progress, or as Paul's letter to the Ephesians puts it 'we are God's work of art' (Ep.2:10). We need to move towards an understanding of the self in terms of relational autonomy[43] which safeguards the importance of individuality as that which exists within a larger and prior relational, interconnected and interdependent context.

An important aspect of this emphasis on human relationality is the underlying affinity and kinship that exists between the human world and the natural world, between the self and the earth, a point emphasised by Pope Francis in *Laudato Si'*. We will return to this point in a moment when we talk of the human as embodied

Dialogue. Closely related to this primacy of relationality is the centrality of dialogue in the genesis, development and fulfilment of the self. Dialogue is a key theme throughout *Laudato Si'*. In the introduction Pope Francis states: 'I would like to enter into dialogue with all people about our common home' (3). He goes on to say what is now needed is 'a new dialogue about how we are shaping the future of our

43. Elizabeth Johnson, *She Who Is: The Mystery of God in Feminist Theological Discourse*, New York: Crossroad, 1992: 154-156.

planet' (14). The encyclical calls for an 'intense' and 'fruitful dialogue' on the relationship between religion and science (62), between ecology and spirituality (Chapter 6), between politics and economics (189-198), as well as a dialogue among religions and equally among the various sciences (201), all in the service of the environment and its well-being. *Laudato Si'*, however, does not propose a philosophy or theology of dialogue; instead it assumes an understanding of dialogue in the spirit of Vatican II, especially as found in *Gaudium et Spes*. What is important here is an appreciation of dialogue as intrinsic to the development of a theological anthropology.

For example, it is only in and through dialogue that we come to know who we are. The self is dialogical in origin: we do not arrive in the world with a ready-made-self. Rather, the self comes to be through dialogical engagement between parents, with parents, and others. Over time the self emerges historically as a work-of-art that is continually under construction, being shaped by a network of relationships and most of all by dialogue. It is in the encounter with others that we are constituted and discover who we are. As Walter Kasper sums up: 'it is in the countenance of the other, in confronting the otherness of others, that we discover ourselves. Not only do we undertake dialogue, we are dialogue'.[44] It is this dialogue with the other that awakens our capacity to be in relationships and to discover, as *Gaudium et Spes* says, that the human is at his or her best in relationship with others, and that it is through a process of 'sincere self-giving' that people 'fully discover themselves' (*GS*, 24). Through dialogue with the other the identity of the

---

44. Walter Kasper, 'Jews, Christians, and the thorny question of mission', *Origins*, vol.32, no.28, 19 December 2002.

self is shaped. Important links exists between dialogue and the development of human identity.

A second equally important dimension to dialogue is its theological foundation in Revelation. One of the key insights of Vatican II is the emphasis on revelation as a dialogical exchange between God and humanity. God has initiated a dialogue with humanity in creation, in the history of Israel and uniquely in the life of Jesus as the face of God to the world. Human beings are invited to participate in this ongoing dialogue in history.

A turning point at the Council was the adoption of dialogue, via Paul VI, especially in *Gaudium et Spes*, as the key to understanding the Church-world relationship and to opening up a new relationship of mutuality between the Church and the world.[45] This shift at the Council required a change of mindset, moving out of a Christendom understanding of Church, abandoning a position of suspicion towards the modern world, and changing over from an exclusively teaching model of church to a teaching and learning model of church. (*GS* 40–44). This development at the Council requires Catholic education to go beyond a preoccupation with handing on the content of the faith as if there was a chemically pure, unalloyed expression of faith. This means moving from a transmission model of Catholic education to a dialogical model in faithfulness to the vision of Vatican II enunciated in the *Decree on Ecumenism* (1964), the *Declaration on Religious Liberty* (1965), the *Declaration on*

45. *Gaudium et Spes*, 40-44. On the importance of mutuality at Vatican II see Dermot A. Lane, 'Keeping the Memory alive: Vatican II as an enduring legacy for Reform of the Church' T, *Vatican II in Ireland, Fifty Years On: Essays in Honour of Padraic Conway*, ed. by Dermot A. Lane, Bern: Peter Lang, 2015:42-44.

the *Relation of the Church to non-Christian Religions* (1965), the *Dogmatic Constitution of Divine Revelation* (1965), and the *Pastoral Constitution on the Church in the Modern World* (1965). It needs to be recognised that handing down the superstructure of Catholicism in creeds and catechisms without dialogical attention to the existential context and experiential agonising of humanity in the twenty-first century will not work and is not working. Without attention to dialogue and inculturation we run the risk of handing on the content of faith without faith. Of course the content of faith and the personal response of faith go together and need each other, but of the two, the personal act of faith is the more important, especially in a questioning culture, and there will always be something of a creative tension between them.

One further point about the dialogical character of humanity is to note that some of the great philosophers of education like Erasmus, Martin Buber and Paolo Freire promoted very successfully a dialogical model of education which has much to offer to Catholic education in the twenty-first century.

Embodiment. A third element in the reconstruction of anthropology for the twenty-first century is the importance of recognising that the self exists only as embodied. Human consciousness, interiority, and subjectivity are only available as embodied; each of these express and communicate themselves through the body.

Neuroscience teaches us that there is an intimate and intricate relationship between mental phenomena and physical phenomena, between activities of the self and the activities of the brain. At the same time, neuroscience denies that the spiritual can be reduced to the physical, or that consciousness can be conflated with the brain. There is something about the self that goes beyond the physical, a sense in which subjectivity is more than matter and yet it is intrinsically connected to and dependent on the body.

We have already alluded to the trend towards 'excarnation' arising from the pervasive influence of technology. The 'I' is never merely a free-floating trace as some postmoderns would have us believe. The 'I' is only available through the body and comes alive when the body is touched. Part of the problem with 'excarnation' is the persistent presence of a dualism that haunts anthropology: body and soul, spirit and matter, self and flesh. This damaging dualism is partly responsible for giving humans the impression that they can dispense with the human body and exploit the body of the earth. One of the strong messages coming through *Laudato Si'* is the link between respect for the human body and respect for the body of the earth.

By way of reaction, Teilhard de Chardin, Rahner and others have argued persuasively for an underlying unity of spirit and matter in an attempt to overcome the dualism that stalks so much anthropology. As far back as 1936 Teilhard de Chardin wrote:

All that exists is matter becoming spirit.

There is neither spirit nor matter in the world;

the stuff of the universe in spirit-matter.

No other substance but this could produce the human molecule.[46]

All matter is spirit-oriented, and as such, is, as it were, spirit frozen in its development. This underlying orientation of matter reaches a unique point of expression in the advent

---

46. Teilhard de Chardin, *Human Energy*, London: Collins, 1969, 57-58.

of the human and finds its fullest realisation in the bodily resurrection of Jesus.

The mechanisation of some forms of modern medicine runs the risk of reducing the body to an item of information such as a particular DNA or a genetic coding or a piece of hardware to be fixed, to the neglect of the body as the primary medium and expression of the self. Such mechanisation of medicine can unintentionally diminish the dignity of the person as an incarnate being.

As embodied, the human is vulnerable to disease, suffering and death. The denial of suffering and death by contemporary culture, especially through the advertising industry, holds out misleading and deceptive promises of earthly perfection and historical fulfilment. When this happens we are no longer operating with a realistic anthropology; instead we are diminishing the human capacity to embrace the inevitability of disease, suffering and death. The US theologian Anthony J. Godiezba reminds us that part of the role of religion is to remind people of their finitude and inbuilt limitations. Being in touch with one's own vulnerability opens us up to the need for each other and the possibility of discerning a deeper dimension to life that we call God.[47] This focus on the human as embodied and vulnerable challenges anthropology in the twenty-first century to go beyond 'the soul-less body of materialistic modernity ... and the body-less soul of a ruthless post-modernity".[48]

---

47. Anthony J. Godzieba, 'Imagination, the Body and the Transformation of Limits', *At the Limits of the Secular: Reflections on Faith and Public Life*, ed. by W. Barbieri, Michigan: W.B. Eerdmans, 2014: 199-225 at 209-210.

48. This terminology is taken from Anthony Kelly, 'The Incarnation and Human Sexuality', *Being Human*, ed.by G. Kirchoffer with R. Horner and P. Mc Ardle, Oregon: Wipf and Stock, 2013:141-155 at 154.

This emphasis on the human as embodied is at the centre of developing what Pope Francis calls 'Human Ecology'. For Francis, it 'is ... our body (that) establishes us in a direct relationship with the environment and other living beings'. So 'learning to accept our body, to care for it and to respect its fullest meaning, is an essential element of any genuine human ecology'. Similarly, Francis notes that 'valuing one's own body in its femininity and masculinity is necessary if I am going to be able to recognise myself in an encounter with someone who is different' (155). Respect for the sexuality, sacredness, and the sacramentality of the human body, for the relationship between the human body and the body of the earth, and for the body of the earth and the cosmos as a part of God's creation, is an essential anthropological ingredient in developing what the new encyclical calls 'Integral Ecology'.

Language. A further ingredient in the construction of anthropology for the twenty-first century is a recognition of the role of language in the constitution of human identity. As human beings we inhabit a world of language which is unique to the human species. We depend on a web of language to discover who we are and how to communicate with each other through this web of language. At a popular level, language is seen as that which describes reality. Language is perceived as instrumental, designed to express and re-present the world as it is. We learn to use language and words for our own ends.

There is, however, another view of language which suggests that language is about discovery, the opening up of an invisible world of meaning, and in particular about the disclosure of who we are and what we do within that world of meaning. There is a sense in which language can use and control us. Within this view, language shapes us and gives us an identity. In this sense, language is constitutive of human identity and contributes to the activation of human agency.

It is through the power of language that human beings are put in touch with each other, enabled to communicate and engage in dialogue. We have already emphasised that humanity is radically relational and dialogical; we now want to suggest that important links exist between language, relationality and dialogue. Language is an important factor in the initiation of dialogue and the development of relationality. Equally, language is a key to the activation of agency and enabling the praxis of self-determination to take place. For a child to survive he or she must become part of a community of language. Initially, the language may be just the cry of a child, sufficient to establish a relationship which subsequently develops verbally. Language, therefore, is not just an add on to human nature; instead language is what constitutes human identity, representing a world of meaning, enabling human agency, and enlarging freedom.

Language has many layers, ranging from the literal to the poetic. The role of education is to open up these many layers and introduce participants to the full range of meaning from the literal to the poetic. The language of revelation, so central to Catholic education, is more akin to poetry than to prose because it is in the poetic mode that language finds its highest possibilities and promises most.[49]

---

49. Michael Scanlon, 'Revelation', *The Modern Catholic Encyclopaedia*, Michael Glazier and Monika K. Helwig (eds.), Dublin: Gill and Macmillan, 1994:747-749 at 748.

No longer living in an anthropocentric universe. A further and final ingredient in the reconstruction of anthropology for Catholic education is the need to go beyond the presence of so much anthropocentrism which is implicit and sometimes explicit in Catholic education and theology. This is a challenge highlighted by the new encyclical (68-69, 115-122) and will require a conscious effort by education and theology to overcome the gap between the natural world and the human world that has been allowed to develop since the Enlightenment. This gap, as the encyclical notes, is one of the root causes of the ecological crisis. As a result of this gap, the human has developed an exaggerated sense of his/her own importance and assumed a licence to exploit the earth.

The current ecological crisis is not only a moral issue, it is also a deeply anthropological and theological issue. As far back as 1967, the scientist Lynn White could write that 'in its western form, Christianity is the most anthropocentric religion the world has seen.'[50] A one-sided reading of *Gaudium et Spes* could certainly give this impression. For example, *Gaudium et Spes* talks about humanity consolidating 'its control over creation' (9) suggesting that 'all things on earth should be related to man as to their centre and crown' (12) and that 'by his interior qualities he out-strips the whole sum of mere things' (14). Further, it says man through 'his intellect surpasses the material universe' and has made great progress 'in his probing of the material world and subjecting it to himself' (15). However, these anthropocentric statements of *Gaudium et Spes* must be balanced by those which talk about 'the dignity of creation and humanity' (41) and the

---

50. Lynn White, 'The Historical Roots of our Ecological Crisis', *Science*, 155, 1967:1205.

participation of creation in salvation (39). It is instructive to remember here that John-Paul II, who had much to say about ecology, talked about an 'anthropological error' in man's 'arbitrary use of the earth, subjecting it without restraint to his will'.[51] Similarly, as we have seen above Francis talks about an inadequate presentation of Christian anthropology as responsible for distorting the relationship between the human and natural world (116).

d. Cosmology, Creation and New Testament Creation-Centred Christologies

The appropriate response to anthropocentrism is not biocentrism, nor is it a reduction of the human to a purely natural phenomenon without distinction and differentiation. Instead, what is needed is an account of the human that recognises the place of the human within the larger and longer story of the cosmos. This, in turn, should be complemented by the Jewish theology of creation found in the Hebrew Scriptures, and by a recovery of creation–centred Christologies of the New Testament. This is not the place to engage in this exercise of *ressourcement*. However, let me briefly indicate the direction such *ressourcement* might take.

We know from contemporary cosmologies that we live in a finely tuned, evolving universe, that began some 13.7 billion years ago. The advent of the human within this timescale is a very recent event. The human exists within this perspective in a delicately balanced relationship of dependence, so much so that scientists tell us that if the

---

51. *Centesimus Annus*, a. 37, 1991, celebrating the hundredth anniversary of *Rerum Novarum*.

rate of expansion one second after the big bang had been different, the universe would have collapsed and the human would not be here today.[52] As we have seen the human exists as embodied consciousness, coming from within the body and not outside it.[53] The human also exists in a unique, embodied relationship with the rest of creation. The human is, as it were, a microcosm of the macrocosm of the universe. Tom Berry, US eco-theologian, kept reminding us that 'we bear the universe in our beings as the universe bears us within its being.'[54]

This understanding of the human within this long cosmic story is often expressed poetically by scientists in the following way: the human is cosmic dust in a state of consciousness, freedom and responsibility. The human exists in a relation of continuity with creation and embodies creation within himself or herself. Brian Swimme, drawing on the revelatory power of poetry, puts it thus: 'The universe shivers with wonder in the depth of the human'[55] or as John Polkinghorne sums up: 'We are all made of the ashes of dead stars'[56] or Elizabeth A. Johnson we are star-stuff and earthdust.[57]

52. S. Hawkings, *A Brief History of Time*, New York: Bantam Books, 1988:121-122. and F. Dyson, *Disturbing Universe*, New York, Harper and Row, 1979: 250.

53. Susan Ross, *Anthropology*, Minnesota: Liturgical Press, 2012, 136-138.

54. Tom Berry, *The Dream of the Earth*, San Francisco: Sierra Club Books, 1988:132.

55. Brian Swimme, *The Universe is a Green Dragon: The Cosmic creation story*, New Mexico: Bear and company, 1984:32).

56. John Polkinghorne, *One World: The Interaction of Science and Theology*, London: SPCK, 1986:56.

57. Elizabeth A. Johnson, *Ask the Beasts: Darwin and the God of Love*, New York: Bloomsbury, 2014: 109.

This view of the human coming from contemporary cosmologies resonates with the Jewish understanding of creation. Two points are worth noting here: it is the breath of Yahweh, that is the Spirit of God, who brings order out of chaos and life out of the dust of the earth and continues to sustain that gift of life in existence. Secondly, within this Jewish theology, *Adam*, the human, is created out of *Adamah*, the earth. Adam, the human, therefore, is better understood as 'an earthling' or 'an earth-creature' or 'an offspring of the earth'. In this, Judaism stresses the intrinsic connection and intimate relationality between the human and the earth which has been lost in modernity.

Turning to the New Testament, it should be noted that the earliest Christologies in Paul are creation-centred, especially the Christologies of Colossians (Col.1:15-29), Ephesians (Ep.1:7-10), Philippians (Phil 2:10-11), and Corinthians(2 Cor.5:9). Further, the confession of Jesus as the Wisdom of God in 1st Corinthians (1Cor. 1:24 and 30) is also a creation-centred Christology, given the role of wisdom within creation in the Hebrew Scriptures (Proverbs 8:22-31).

Within this vision of the early New Testament creation-centred Christologies, we begin to see a close link between creation and Incarnation. Creation is the basis of Incarnation and Incarnation is the fulfilment of creation.[58] Put in contemporary terms we might begin to see Christology as 'concentrated creation': what happens in Christology is a crystallisation of the drama taking place in creation. It is this intimate relationship between the natural world and the human, between creation and Incarnation, between

---

58. Dermot A. Lane, *The Reality of Jesus: An Essay in Christology*, Dublin: Veritas, 1975: 134-145.

nature and grace that should become the basis of a new anthropology informing Catholic education and theology.

Let me conclude by giving the last word to Gerard Manley Hopkins who captures, ahead of his time in 1918, this new anthropology in the poem 'Ribblesdale':

'And what is earth's eye, tongue or heart else
Where else but in dear dogged man'.

In brief, therefore, we are suggesting that the reconstruction of anthropology in the twenty-first century should go beyond modern anthropocentrism and seek to include at least reference to the importance of the human as relational, dialogical, embodied, linguistic, and creation-centred. These perspectives along with the structural shifts of Vatican II and the horizons opened up by *Laudato Si'* should become hallmarks of Catholic education in the twenty-first century.

CONCLUSION

These reflections on Catholic education in the light of Vatican II and *Laudato Si'* suggest that the self-understanding of Catholicism, and therefore of Catholic education, has developed over the last fifty years. Vatican II effected a number of shifts that touch on the way Catholic education will conduct itself in the twenty-first century:

- a new openness to the world
- a church that not only teaches but is also prepared to learn from the world through dialogue
- a commitment to ecumenical dialogue as a part of Catholic identity
- a recognition of the 'elements of truth and grace' as well as the presence of 'seeds of the Word' in other religions
- an appreciation of the importance of anthropology in theology and education.

Similarly, *Laudato Si'* has opened up new horizons on understanding the global responsibility of all to reduce man-made climate change and to hear the cry of the earth and of the poor. These ethical and moral challenges are a matter of justice between the nations and the generations.

To implement all these new horizons *Laudato Si'* commits the Church:

- to moving beyond an anthropocentric view of the universe
- to promoting ecological education as a part of Catholic education
- to working towards ecological conversion as a key outcome of Catholic education.

These developments at Vatican II and in *Laudato Si'* are not optional extras in Catholic education. Instead they are an intrinsic part of what it means to be Catholic in the twenty-first century and are, therefore, at the core of Catholic education.[*]

---

[*] This essay is an expanded version of a lecture on 'Vatican II and New Thinking about Catholic Education', given at an international conference in Heythrop College, London, 23 - 24 Jun 2015, marking the fiftieth anniversary of *Gravissium Educationis*.